A skyline to warm the heart of every Sunderland fan.

Dedicated to Charles Biggs Snr and Adam King

Acknowledgments

We wish to thank all those, without whose help and support, this book could not have been published.

Northern Arts
Sunderland AFC Directors, Players,
Management and Ground Staff
Mailcom plc
Alec King Consultancies
Homeworthy Furniture
Stewart Hindmarsh Advertising

First published in Great Britain by
Cedar Lodge Marketing Limited, Ashbrooke, Sunderland SR2 7TW
Photoworks
ISBN 0951 701 606
Sunderland AFC 100th Year Book (bbk)

Produced by Stewart Hindmarsh Advertising Limited, Cedars Lodge, The Cedars,
Ashbrooke, Sunderland SR2 7TW
Printed by Baker Brothers Litho Limited, Monkhill Lane, Pontefract,
West Yorkshire WF8 1RW

Sunderland AFC's 100th year in the football league, could have been written by a thriller novelist, so full was it of excitement, disapointment, drama and celebration. It has been our privilege to photograph the most exciting and intimate of these moments capturing them for future generations of Sunderland supporters.

Photographs by Charles Biggs & Alice King.

Instant happiness for 35,000.

FOREWORD
BY
JAMES
HERRIOT

It is a fair old drive from Thirsk to Roker but James Herriott is a regular attender at home matches. Here he shares his passion for the club.

Looking back over my life I can see that there was no way I could have avoided being a Sunderland fanatic unless somebody had got to me before the age of three, but my father had brain-washed me long before that.

He was a Sunderland man whose work took him to Glasgow in 1916 and I was whisked off to that city as a three week old baby.

He liked Scotland, but it broke his heart to be separated from his beloved football team. He had grown up in the great days of the club in the eighteen nineties and the early nineteen hundreds. Five times league champions, crammed with international players, recognised as the "Team of all talents," the undisputed glamour club of the era.

To my father, Rangers and Celtic were poor substitutes and he worked off his frustrations on me. He never taught me nursery rhymes, instead he taught me to recite the great teams he had watched over the years at Roker Park. My childish brain swam with the names of Buchan, Holley, Mordue, Cuggy and countless others and one of his great joys was to recount, kick by kick, some of the great names of the past. I don't know how many times I heard about the time when Sunderland defeated Newcastle 9-1 at St James' Park - it had happened many years before I was born, but could I describe the whole ninety minutes.

Saturday nights were fraught with suspense. How had those far-off Sunderland lads fared? I remember so vividly, as a child in the days even before radio, tremblingly opening the pages of the Glasgow Evening Times and running my finger down the football results. It was just about that time that I stopped enjoying my Saturday tea when our team had lost and that situation hasn't changed all that much even though I am now in my seventies.

Through my father's promptings the Sunderland players gradually assumed the status of Gods and I could hardly comprehend the possibility of actually viewing these fabled creatures in the flesh.

Since I lived so far away this didn't happen till I had reached the age of nine. It was 1925 and my parents had taken me through to Sunderland to visit relatives. I broke away from the family party, ran round to Roker Park and when the gates opened for the last ten minutes I climbed up breathlessly onto the terraces and the very moment when I breasted the stairs and glimpsed the sacred turf for the first time, Dave Halliday burst through the middle and crashed a tremendous shot into the net, one of the forty-two goals he scored that season. That was the final clincher. I stood entranced for those ten minutes feeling a lifting of the heart at the very sight of the red and white stripes - a feeling which has never left me.

It was a strange coincidence that when I qualified as a veterinary surgeon I worked for a while in Sunderland, and when I went to my very first case the old farmer looked at me gloomily and said "Another bloody Scotchman." With my thick Clydeside accent it was no good trying to tell him that I had been born a couple of hundred yards from the Roker Park ground, but I did manage to get the conversation round to football.

The farmer was a keen fan and was thunderstruck when I was able to chat knowledgeably about the players and matches of fifty years ago. My fame soon spread. All the farmers seemed to be Sunderland supporters and they were agog at the idea of this young Scot who had an encyclopedic knowledge of their club's history. Little throw-away lines like, "I've always thought the Doig, McCombie and Watson defence of the 1900-01 season was one of the best which ever played for Sunderland" or "Those were two fine goals Arthur Bridgett scored in the second half against Newcastle in 1908" really sent their eyebrows up.

I didn't have to be a brilliant vet - I was made.

And now, when I live only fifty odd miles away and can see the old team regularly, I feel that life has not a great deal more to offer. I have suffered along with my Roker Park brothers, but we have never been bored. And, in 1973 when the referee blew the final whistle at Wembley and I found myself dancing with my arms around a distinguished looking elderly gentleman in a camel coat who was a total stranger, I felt that from that moment on I could die happy. Some people would say it's all silly - but not my father.

As I turn the pages of this book I wish such a thing could have been available long ago. My father's football idols and mine at an early age are shadowy figures and the pictures which depict them are often poor and indistinct. In fact, many of them are enshrined only in memory. It would be wonderful if great players of the past like Charlie Buchan and Dave Halliday could have been brought to life by the brilliant photography of Alice King and Charles Biggs.

It is a dream which can never be realised but this compilation of pictures provides a deeply satisfying consolation. I am, today, even more of a Sunderland fan than I was in my early life and it is a happy thought that the present Roker heroes have been caught in their prime and preserved for all time in these superb photographs.

The collection is a football lover's treasure house and is unique in that it shows our players as few have seen them - in their homes, with their families, in happy, unguarded moments. And I would like to think that in the far future, supporters like me will open this book and point to pictures of young footballers who have become world famous and say "Look, there are the lads, exactly as I remember them!"

A MESSAGE FROM THE CHAIRMAN

In Sunderland AFC's Centenary Season as members of the Football League, it is pleasing that this unique and quality work has been published on our great football club.

This book reflects various aspects of a Big Club and features many of the positive areas of our game. It will prove of interest, not only to dedicated Sunderland AFC supporters, but to everyone who enjoys both football and photography. Those people fortunate enough to have purchased this book will no doubt enjoy reviewing it constantly in future years.

I was lucky enough to have been born a Sunderland supporter, as was my father before me. Coming from a Sunderland

family I have followed the fortunes of the club from the terraces for 36 years. I have had my heroes and idols, disappointments and treasured memories, but football is more exciting now with pace and skill so much to the forefront, as this work now illustrates.

The fact that this club enjoys the Division One status it did one hundred years ago is most commendable, not only to the people currently at the club, but to our forefathers.

Numerous changes have taken place over the last 100 years and it would have been impossible to foresee the deep affection that our national game has captured over this period of time.

Sunderland AFC is the focal point for over one million people, and in addition to representing this great town, the club is recognised through football as having a large volume of quality, knowledgeable and respected supporters. The future will no doubt throw many challenges our way, however, with the depth of feeling and the love and devotion the club enjoys, I feel sure we will continue to succeed.

I view my privileged position as Chairman as one only of trusteeship. This responsibility means working with others for the continuing success of the club which is so important to the area in so many ways.

Bob Murray

BOB MURRAY
CHAIRMAN

Introduction

A chance meeting on a Photography course in 1987, brought together Charles Biggs and Alice King. During casual conversation, Alice informed Charles of her husband's role as Commercial Manager of Sunderland AFC. Charles, a supporter of the team for many years, had always wanted to take portraits of the players and asked Alice if she could help gain permission. Alice helped arranged this and Charles began on his project.

Alice too, had in her mind a project to photograph those unseen moments around Roker Park to capture the incredible atmosphere that surrounds this historic stadium. The two discussed both projects culminating in the suggestion of producing this book which portrays the 100th year of Sunderland Football Club in the Football League.

The two now had the idea, the location and the subject matter to start their book. A presentation of work was made to Northern Arts and a photographic award was given to Charles and Alice. Work began in earnest in late 1987 on the absorbing task which lay ahead.

From the outset, the plan was to record the private side of these very public people. It took time for the photographers to gain total confidence of the players and staff, so that they got used to performing naturally and ignoring the focussed lens on their activities. However, as time progressed, everyone at Roker accepted and trusted Charles and Alice, enabling them to capture these memorable studies.

Neither one new what lay ahead, and if they had, they're sure this book would not have been published. But with tenacity and application and on many occasions going cold, wet and hungry, the material gradually accrued. The photographs were taken on several different formats of camera which they feel have added extra dimensions to the finished work.

Their determination can be seen in the photographs and their supreme quality. As the project progressed, stresses and clashes naturally occurred; however, a bond was formed which saw them through to their common aim, the publication of these photographs printed in a Fine Arts Book format. Indeed, both Charles and Alice agree that many of the best images were taken during times of growing tension between the two.

Everyone who has viewed the material is delighted with its quality and presentation, and through this fine book, the work of Charles Biggs and Alice King, but more importantly, the 100th year of Sunderland Football Club in the Football League will live on so that future supporters can see their heroes as they were, in years to come.

Images Around the Ground

Roker Park is a shrine to Sunderland AFC supporters. The unique atmosphere created by the supporters and ground has over the years won many extra points for the team. A very large, yet intimate building, it has seldom, if ever, been seen in this format.

The famous club mascot, the Black Cat

MARSHALL
394
BRANSON
ZITAIR
100
SAFC
WEED

The Programme sellers trolley

Gary, the youngest head groundsman in the football league

Still three hours to kick off

Roker Park Suite

Sunderland's Club historian, Billy Simmons

This young supporter's 'having a ball' at the new club shop

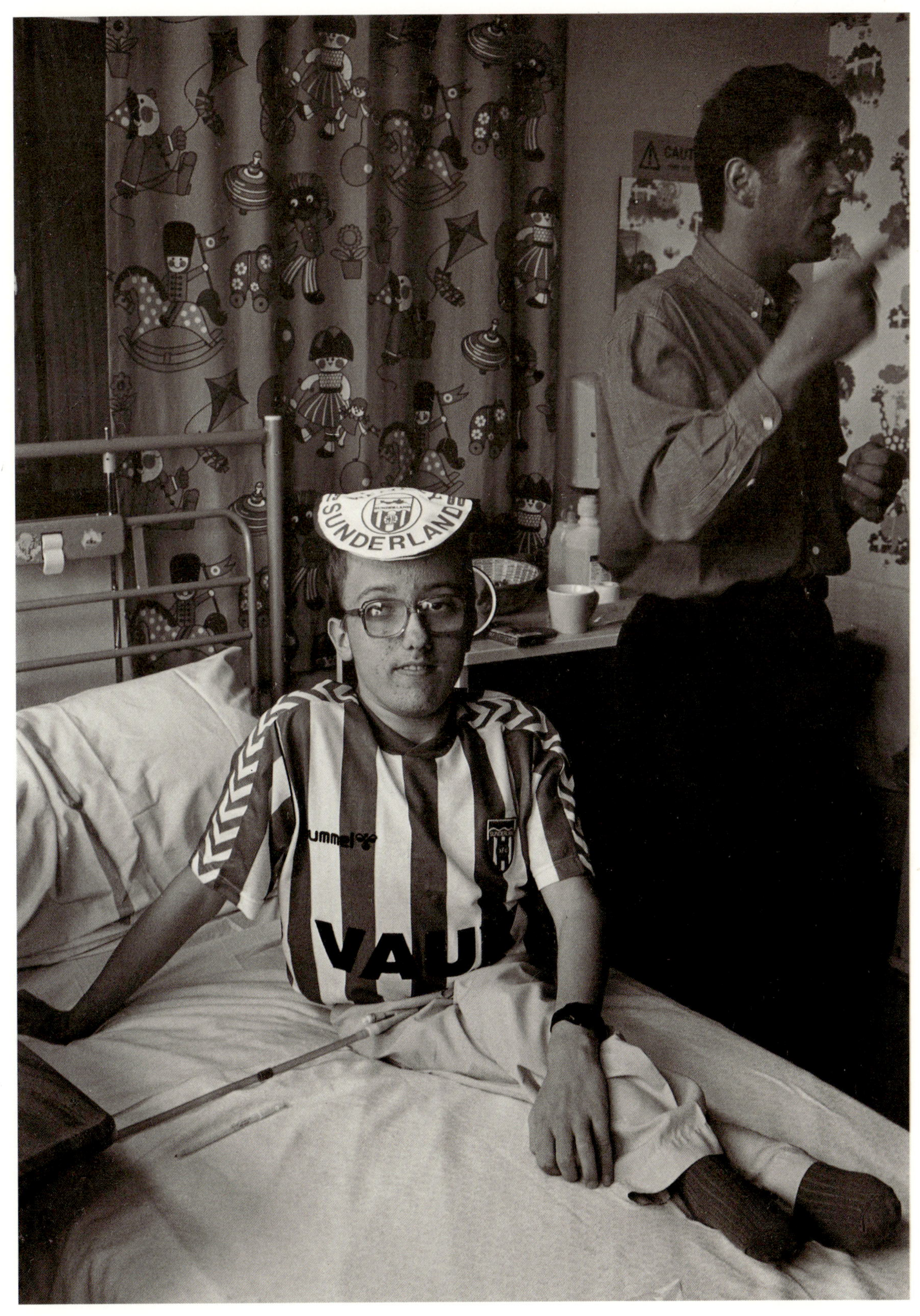

John McPhail visits a supporter in the town's General Hospital

NIKE
AU

Club supporters

Roker Park

St Johns Ambulance men

A very young supporter

EXIT

Goalkeepers Tony Norman and Tim Carter

The Wearside Football Festival

Victory in the semi-final of the Wearside Football Festival

Sumo wrestlers a possible new half time attraction

Supporters at open day

Kieron Brady at the International Wearside Football Festival

Every year the Clubs open day attracts thousands

Jimmy Montgomery can still keep them out

Charlie Hurley opens the clubs new training ground

Sir Stanley Mathews opens the Wearside Football Festival

A native Wearsider, Kate Adie

Young supporters cycle miles to see their heroes training

SFC 4P

Like so many ideas, the Roker Rover was another league first for the Club

The Roker Rover adds even more colour to the famous Durham Miners Gala

Thousands of Sunderland's famous black cat mascots were sold during the play offs

Law and Order

Soccer has now lost its 'hooligan' image with much thanks to the excellent behaviour of players during the 1990 World Cup. Sunderland AFC plays a vital role in the community. Known affectionately as the 'caring club', it has formed strong links with the police, correctional and educational facilities, constantly telling the Roker message of "Soccer is for the enjoyment of all the family".

NR NORTHERN ROCK

Pre-match briefing

Their biggest worry is what the scoreline will be

DAY
TOF
YS

Police constable stepping through gate 5

The Clubs Hillsborough memorial service

Deerbolt young offenders prison

In the carpentry shop

The engineering shop

The players and inmates share football stories

The players and inmates share football stories

The Action

What a year of action it was. Promotion challengers, play off finalists at Wembley and ultimately promotion to the First Division. Some great games including victory over arch rivals Newcastle United.

Gary Bennett stretching every sinue

Pre-season training is tough, particularly on a hot, summers day

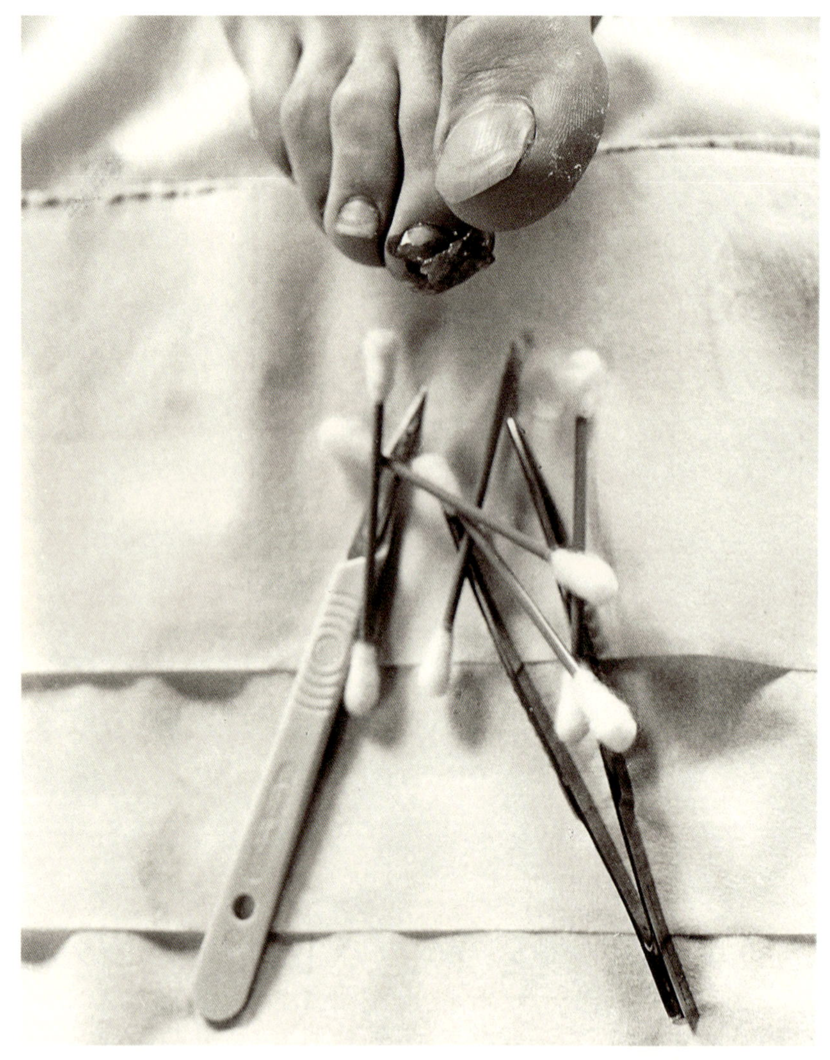

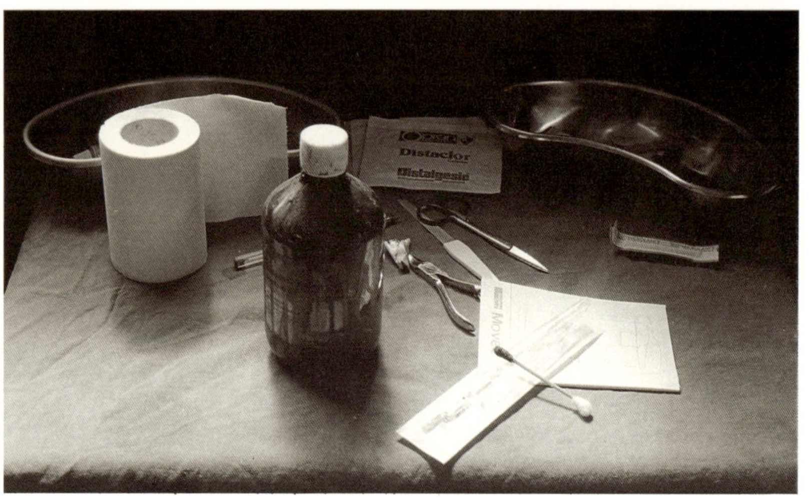

In the treatment room

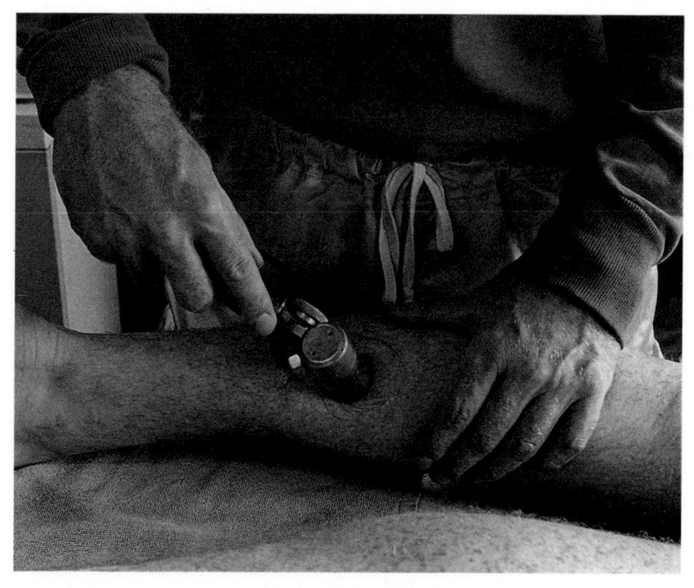

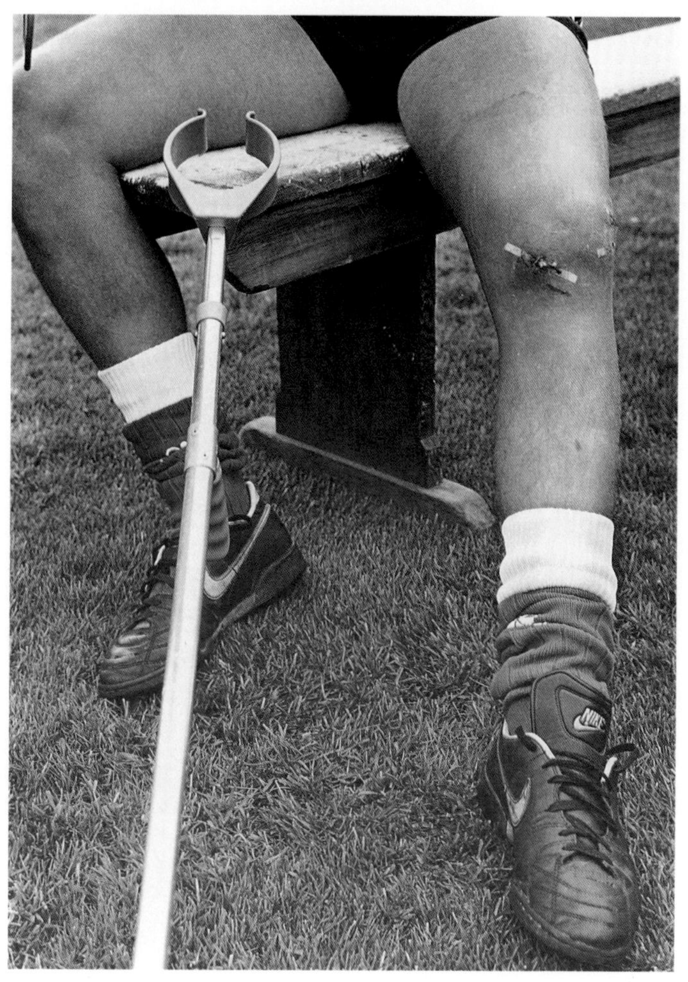

Injuries are an occupational hazard

The boot room

The joy of scoring

Close marking is a facet of todays game, here it is applied to Thomas Hauser

A unique view of Roker

a) control on the ball

b) the actions fast and furious

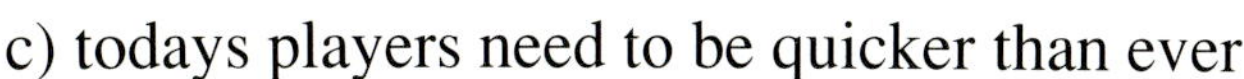
c) todays players need to be quicker than ever

d) balance and good reflexes are a must

Gary Owers

Tony Norman

VAUX
Apollo 2000

Training at Whitburn

Newcastle Manager, Jim Smith during the play offs

Peter Davenport and Neville Southall

Marco in action

FIRST HALF
VAUX
VAUX BREWERIES
VAUX
SECOND HALF
ATTACK
UNIVERSAL SEALANTS (UK) LTD
USL
091 - 4161530.

Attack!

Sunderland take the lead in a decisive play off 'Derby' against Newcastle United

Colin Pascoe

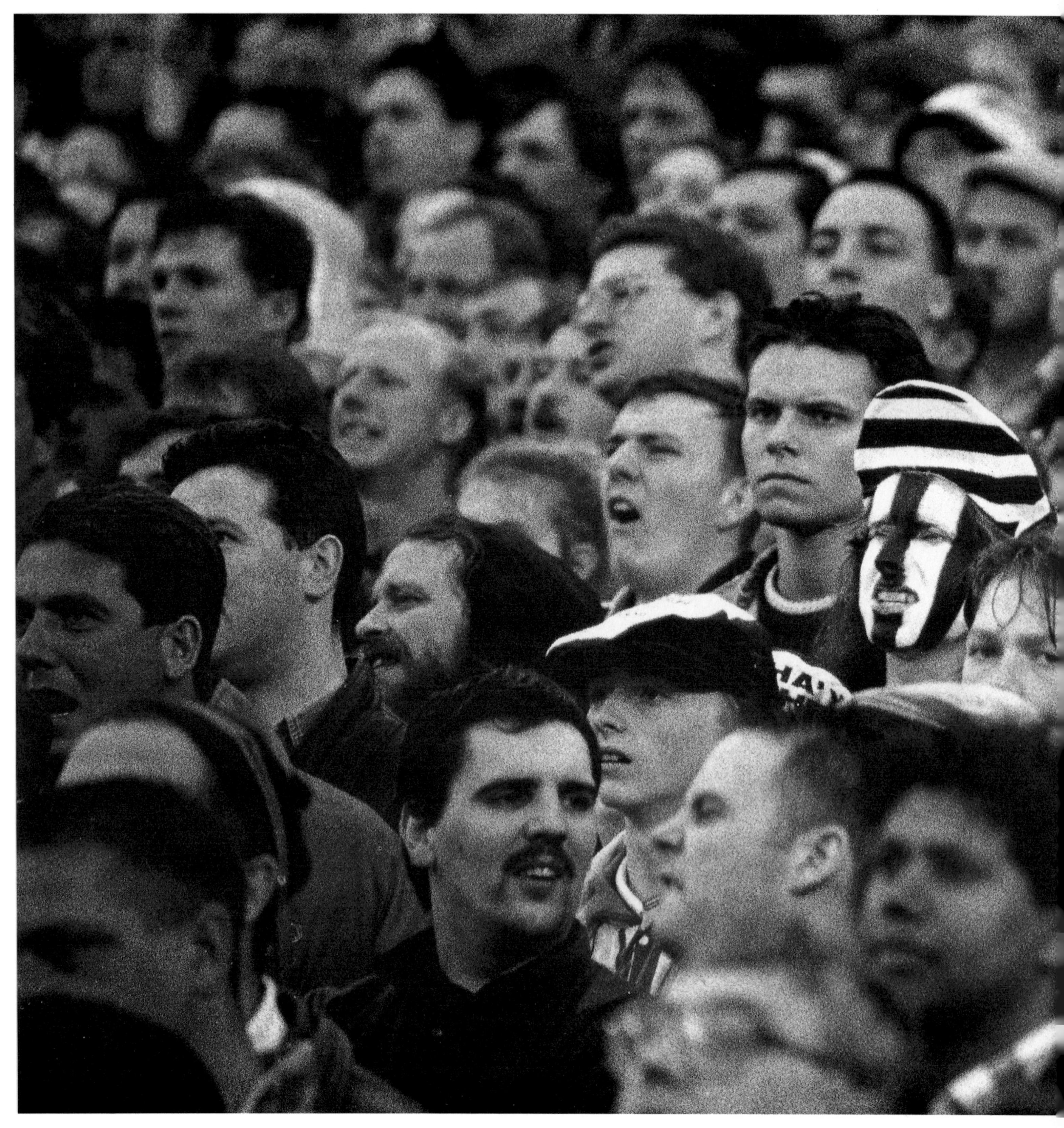

This striped faced supporter shows the tension

Gary in full flight

Gazza and Marco

Eric Gates with referee, George Courteney

The Players

To thousands they are heroes, to a handful they are friends and to special individuals they are fathers, sons, grandsons and husbands. These photographs capture the private people, those unseen relaxed moments onand off the pitch.

Youth Team line ups

At home on soccer pitch or cricket ground, Richard Ord

Michael Heathcoate enjoying breakfast in the Bungalow Cafe

Brian Atkinsons' ability has led to first team appearances

Jerseyman, Jonathan Trigg and Kieron Brady from Glasgow

Local hero John Kay and Irelands' Tommy Lynch

Gary Bennett

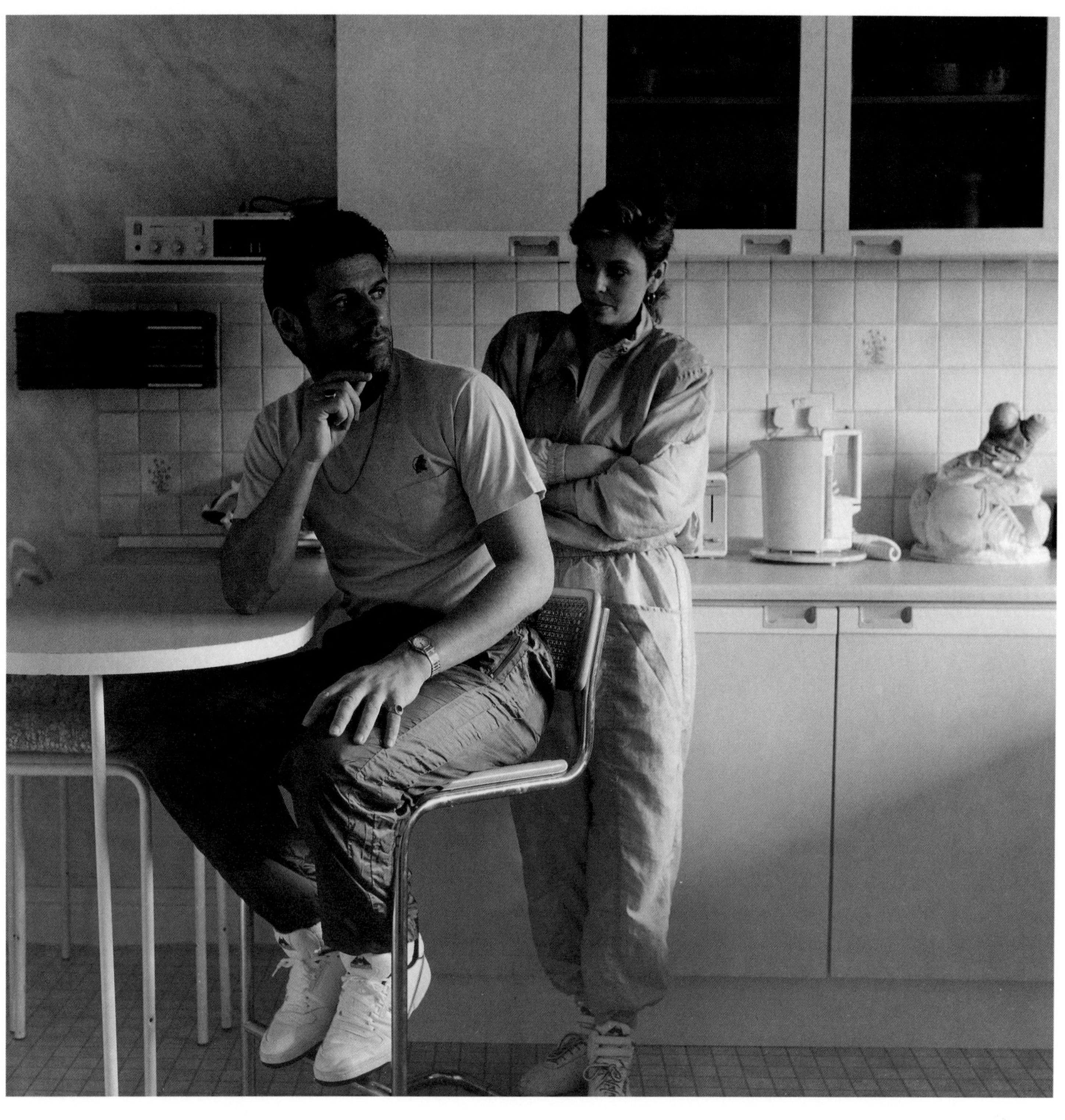

John McPhail and his wife in their Teesside home

Rueben Agboola pictured in Bobby Kerrs', Hastings Hill pub

That football fever permeates to the young office staff

Richard Ords' grandfather

Peter Davenport and wife relax at home

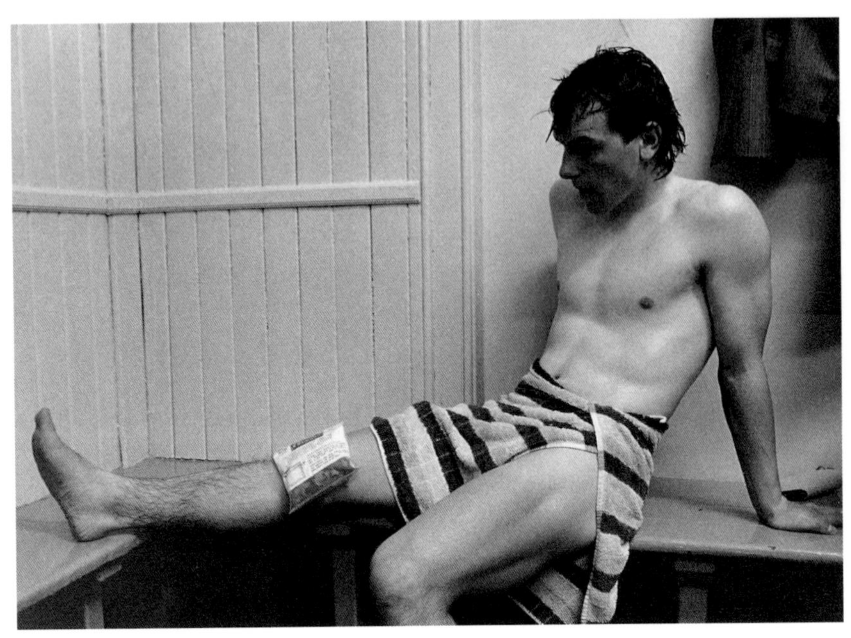

Paul Hardyman and son

Gordon Armstrong and his younger brother

Gordon Armstrong and family

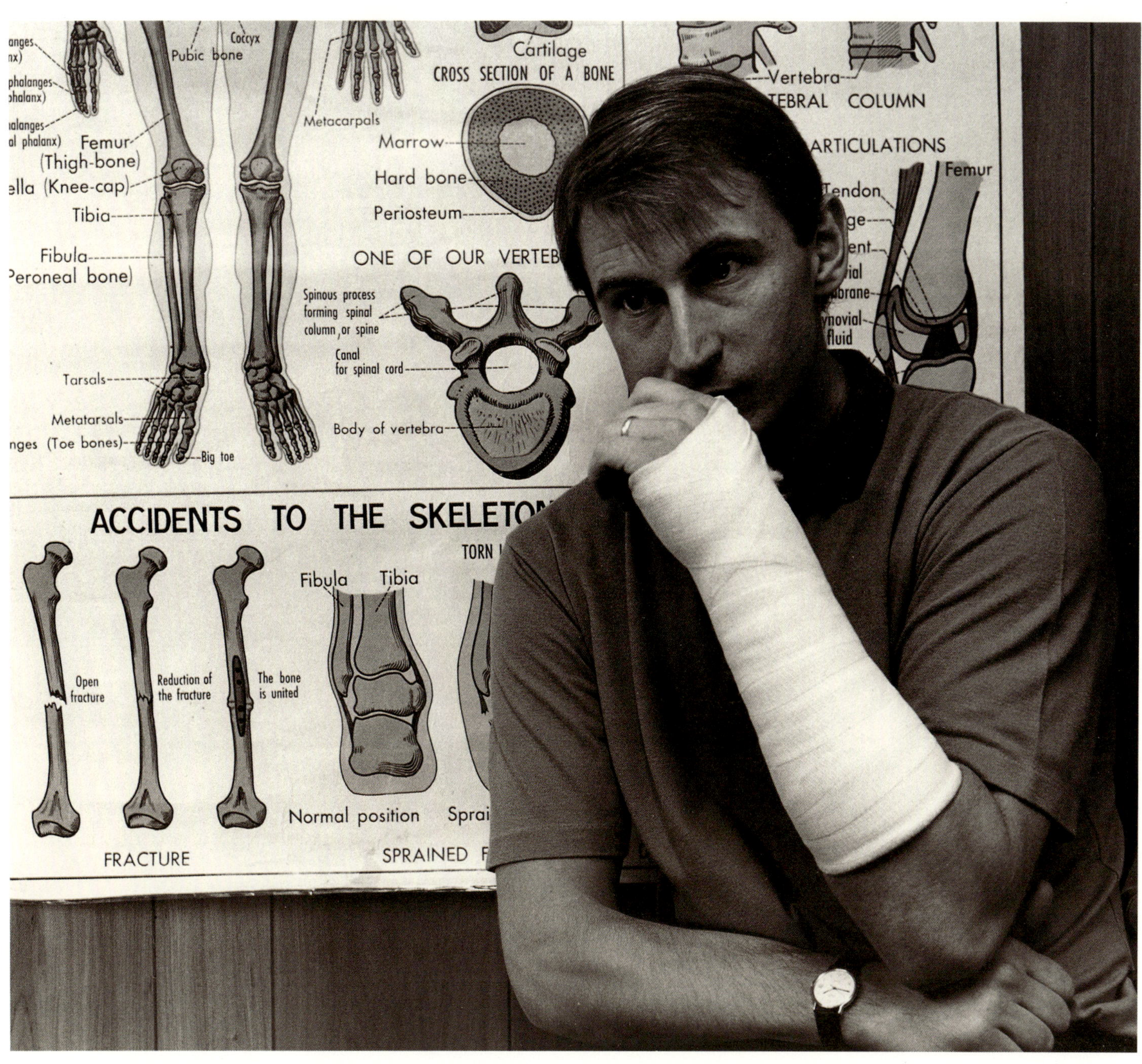

Coccyx
Pubic bone
Cartilage
CROSS SECTION OF A BONE
Vertebra
Metacarpals
Marrow
Hard bone
Periosteum
Femur
(Thigh-bone)
Tibia
Fibula
Tendon
Femur
ARTICULATIONS
fluid
Spinous process forming spinal column, or spine
Canal for spinal cord
Body of vertebra
Tarsals
Metatarsals
Big toe
ACCIDENTS TO THE SKELETO
Fibula
Tibia
Open fracture
Reduction of the fracture
The bone is united
Normal position
FRACTURE

Warren Hawke

THE
WORLD

Tony Norman

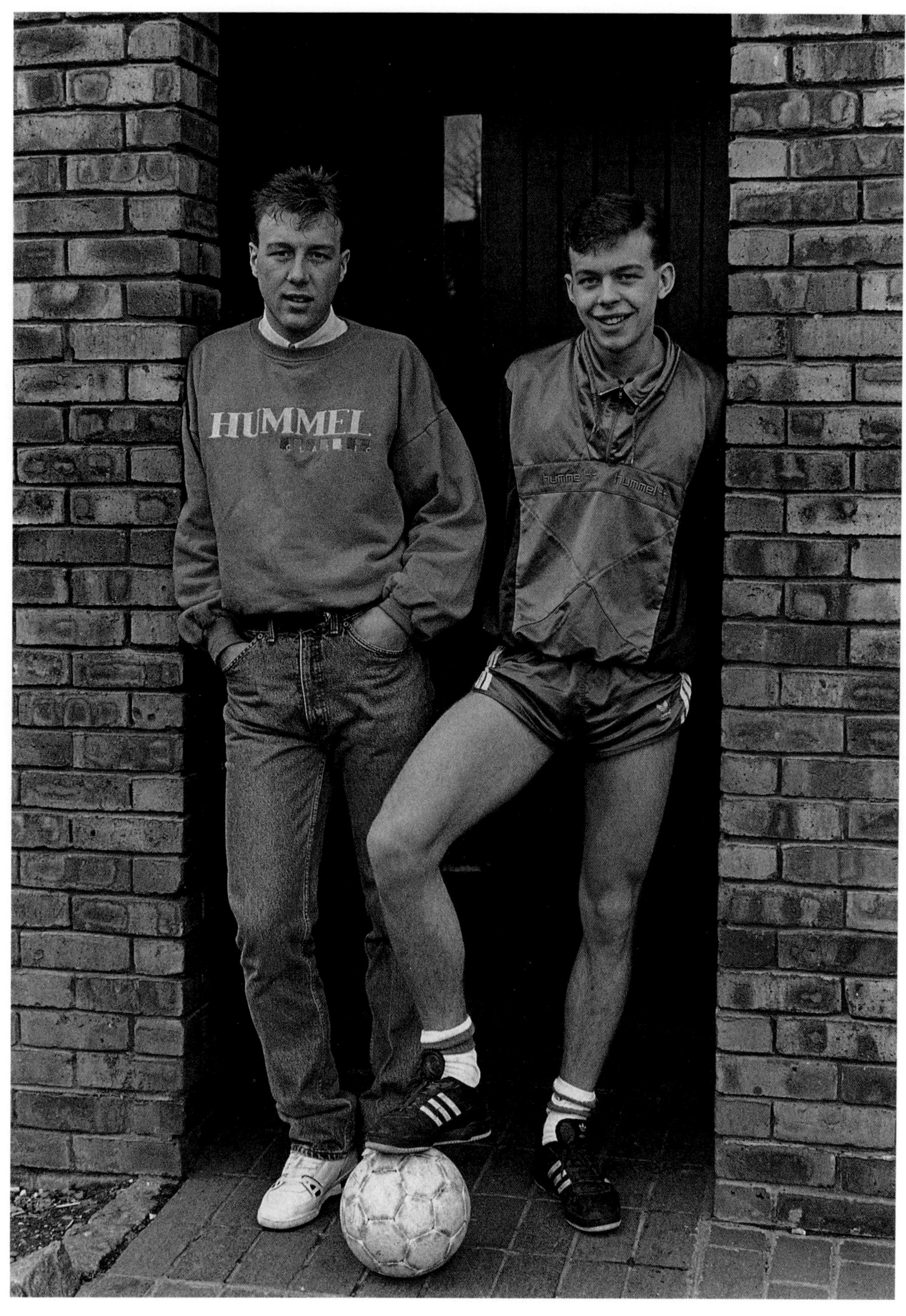

Gary Owers and younger brother

Eric inherited his keen interest in pigeons from his father

Eric Gates with Snowy

ASHINGTON
A.F.C.

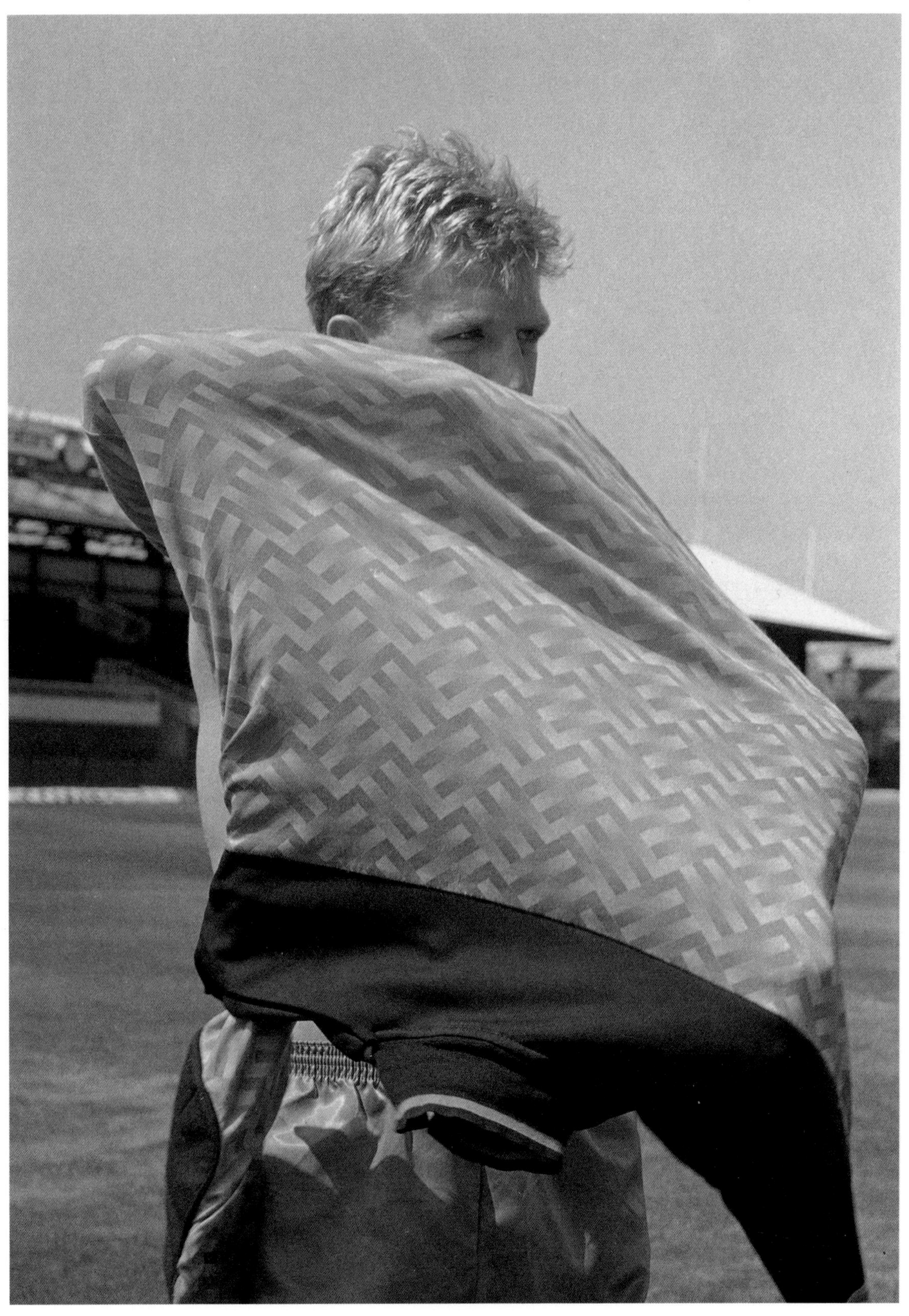

A striking family resemblance, the Gabbiadini brothers, Marco and Ricardo

Mrs Gabbiadini and her two sons

Gordon Armstrong being interviewed

A captain close up

Thomas Hauser on red nose day

Wembley

To most clubs and players, a Wembley appearance is their ultimate goal. It has, without doubt, no equal in the game of soccer.

Counsellor Andrew Myers, Mayor of Sunderland

Rueben Agboola

The players wives and girlfriends

Gary Owers at Wembley stadium. (photo by Club Doctor A J Crummie)

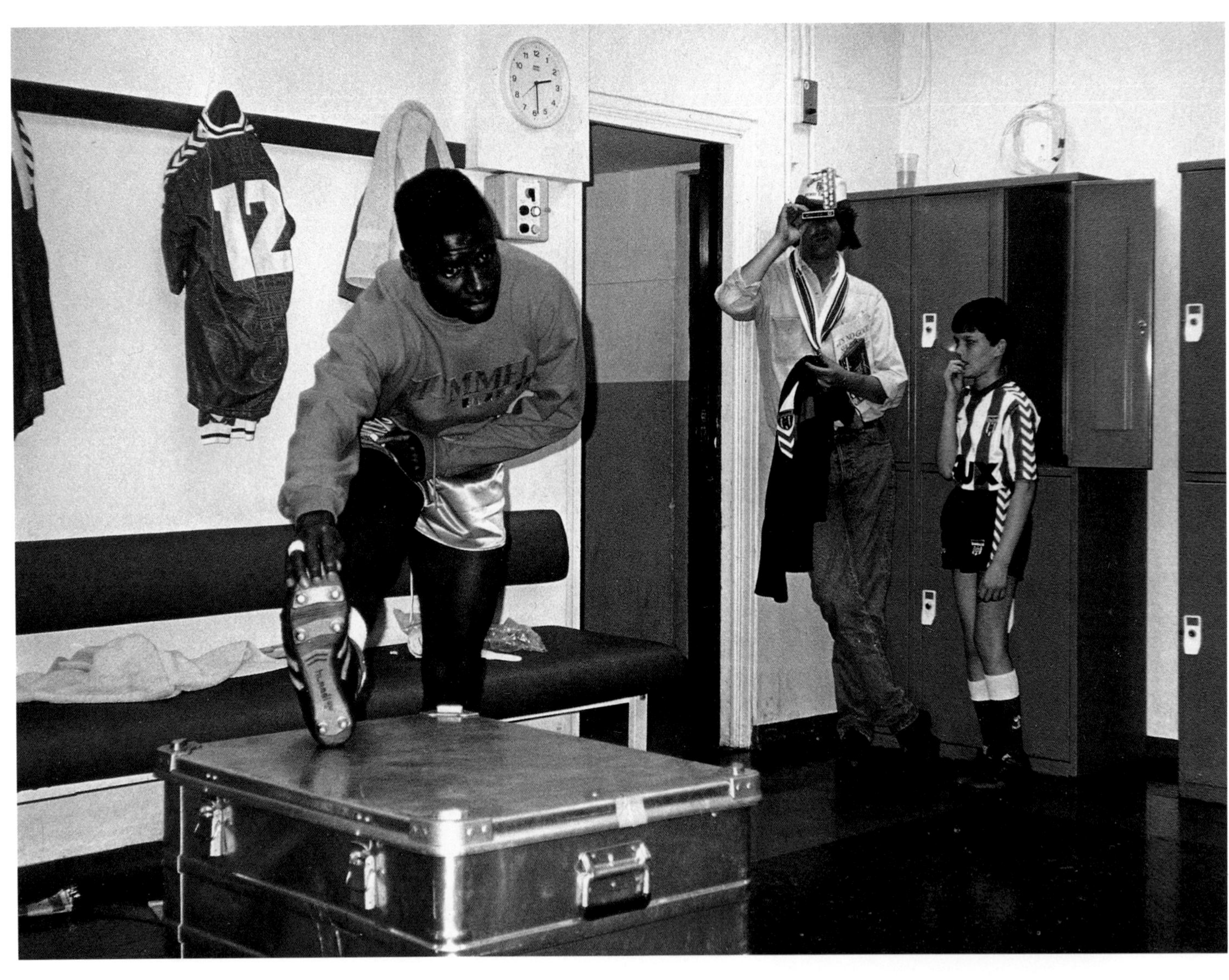

The Wembley mascot (photo by Club Doctor A J Crummie)

Chairman, Bob Murray

Wembley appearance

Sunderland at Wembley

SAFC

hummel
VAUX
hummel
VAUX
1990
WEMBLEY
SUNDERLAND
S·A·F·C
VAUX

Motivation and consolation are both important parts of a coaches job

John McPhail

The Manager

In four short years Dennis Smith has taken Sunderland from the Third to the First Division and his new contract will see him become the Club's longest serving Post War Manager. Stoke born and bred his professional career started with his home town club for which he played over 500 games and won a Football League Cup Winners Medal in 1972. His management style is meticulous, his decisions carefully considered and his success well deserved.

Denis, wife Kate and son Thomas

Len Whites testimonial game at Whitley bay

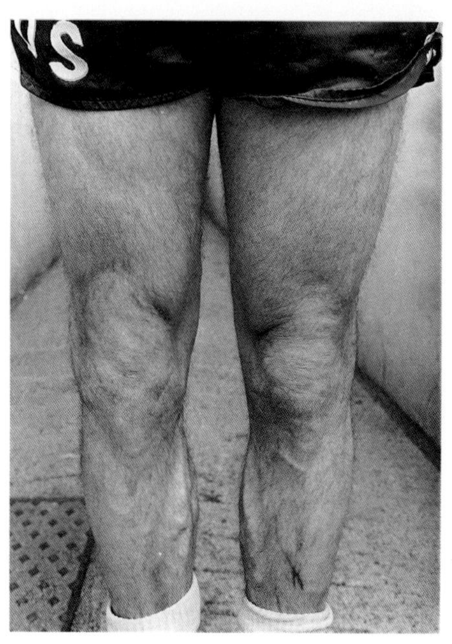

The Beginning

Already Sunderland AFC are into their 101st season, successfully competing in the worlds greatest football league.

INDEX TO PHOTOGRAPHS

Page

35 Roker end before the game.

36 Untitled.

37 Pre-match briefing.

38 Fulwell end.

39 Fulwell end.

40 Police constable stepping through gate 5.

41 The Clubs Hillsborough memorial service.

42 Deerbolt young offenders prison. First team players visited inmates as the highlight of Princes Trust week.

43 In the carpentry shop.

44 The engineering shop.

45 The players and inmates share football stories.

46 The players and inmates share football stories.

47 Marco on the ball.

48 Gary Bennett stretching every sinue.

49 Pre-season training is tough, particularly on a hot, humid summers day.

50 In the treatment room.

51 Injuries are an occupational hazard.

52 The boot room.

53 This one says it all, the joy of scoring a goal captured at its crescendo.

54 Close marking is a facet of todays game, here it is applied to Thomas Hauser.

55 Paul Hardyman

56 A unique view of Roker.

Page

57 a) control on the ball
b) the action's fast and furious
c) players need to be quicker than ever
d) balance and good reflexes are a must

58 Gary Owers.

59 Tony Norman.

60 The agony of a missed penalty.

West Brom away game.

61 Training at Whitburn.

62 Newcastle Manager, Jim Smith during the play offs.

63 Peter Davenport and Neville Southall share a joke during the Everton game.

64 Marco in action.

65 Attack!

66 How quickly fortunes change in the game of football as Sunderland take the lead in a decisive play off 'Derby' against arch rivals Newcastle United.

67 Former Roker junior, Watford's Wilf Rostron, challenges Colin Pascoe for the ball.

68 This striped faced supporter shows the tension.

70 Gary in full flight.

71 Two of todays big stars, Gazza and Marco.

72 Eric Gates shares a joke with one of the games best known referees, George Courteney.

73 Photo call.

74 Youth team line ups.

75 At home on soccer pitch or cricket ground, Richard Ord enjoys his closed season playing for Murton.

76 Michael Heathcoate enjoying breakfast in the Bungalow Cafe which overlooks the bracing North Sea.

Page

77 Recognised as a Club with one of the best youth policies in the game, local lad Brian Atkinsons' determination, skill and ability has already been rewarded with first team appearances.

78 Jerseyman Jonathan Trigg, and Kieron Brady from Glasgow survey the arena that will, they hope, launch their successful soccer careers.

79 John Kay and Ireland's Tommy Lynch.

80 A portrait of Gary Bennett.

81 John McPhail and his wife in their Teesside home.

82 Rueben Agboola pictured in Bobby Kerr's Hastings Hill pub which features great pictures from the famous 1973 Cup Final.

83 Football fever permeates to the young office staff who dream of one day playing on the Roker turf.

84 Richard Ord's grandfather remembers the days when every Murton family was connected with Coal Mining.

85 Peter and Lesley Davenport relax at home in their conservatory.

86 Meditation or medication, both are needed after a tough game.

87 Paul Hardyman and son - purveyors a fine football.

Gordon Armstrong and his younger brother relax at their home near Newcastle.

88 Gordon Armstrong and family.

89 Tony Norman.

90 Warren Hawke looks forward to seeing his name in lights. These particular ones are part of the fabulous Sunderland Illuminations.

91 Card game - John McPhail and Eric Gates.

92 Tony Norman.

Page

93 Gary Owers and younger brother.

94 Eric inherited his keen interest in pigeons from his father.

95 Eric Gates with Snowy.

96 Many Saturday nights are spent on Britains motorways.

97 Marco and Mirandinia at Ashington AFC.

Marco.

98 Marco.

99 Marco cover up.

100 A striking family resemblance, the Gabbiadini brothers, Marco and Ricardo.

101 Mrs Gabbiadini enjoys painting in water colours and following the careers of her two sons.

102 Thomas Hauser enjoying some comic relief on red nose day.

a) Gordon Armstrong being interviewed in the 'dug out'.
b) a captain close up.

103 The Wembley twin towers, a sign of success.

104 Counsellor Andrew Myers, Mayor of Sunderland and Roker supporter.

105 Rueben Agboola.

106 The team behind the team, the players wives and girlfriends play an important role in the success of the Club.

107 Gary Owers at Wembley Stadium.
(photo by Club Doctor A J Crummie)

108 The Wembley mascot .
(photo by Club Doctor A J Crummie)

109 In the Jacuzzi.

110 Viv consoles his daughter .

First published in Great Britain by
Cedar Lodge Marketing Limited, Ashbrooke, Sunderland SR2 7TW
Photoworks
ISBN 0951 701 606
Sunderland AFC 100th Year Book (bbk)

Produced by Stewart Hindmarsh Advertising Limited, Cedars Lodge, The Cedars, Ashbrooke, Sunderland SR2 7TW
Printed by Baker Brothers Litho Limited, Monkhill Lane, Pontefract, West Yorkshire WF8 1RW

First published in 1990